STEPPING STONES FOR CAREGIVERS

NAVIGATING THE MENTAL AND EMOTIONAL TRAUMA OF CAREGIVING

KAREN LEEMAN

BALBOA.PRESS

A DIVISION OF HAY HOUSE

Balboa Press books may be ordered through booksellers or by contacting:

Balboa Press
A Division of Hay House
1663 Liberty Drive
Bloomington, IN 47403
www.balboapress.com
844-682-1282

Because of the dynamic nature of the Internet, any web addresses or
links contained in this book may have changed since publication and
may no longer be valid. The views expressed in this work are solely those
of the author and do not necessarily reflect the views of the publisher,
and the publisher hereby disclaims any responsibility for them.

The author of this book does not dispense medical advice or prescribe the use
of any technique as a form of treatment for physical, emotional, or medical
problems without the advice of a physician, either directly or indirectly. The
intent of the author is only to offer information of a general nature to help
you in your quest for emotional and spiritual well-being. In the event you use
any of the information in this book for yourself, which is your constitutional
right, the author and the publisher assume no responsibility for your actions.

Any people depicted in stock imagery provided by Getty Images are
models, and such images are being used for illustrative purposes only.
Certain stock imagery © Getty Images.

Print information available on the last page.

ISBN: 979-8-7652-5256-7 (sc)
ISBN: 979-8-7652-5255-0 (e)

Library of Congress Control Number: 2024916112

Balboa Press rev. date: 08/07/2024

*To my spouse, children, parents, and family
for their steadfast love and belief.*

CONTENTS

PREFACE

As an informal caregiver, I have the privilege of connecting with other informal caregivers. Though their situations are unique, I am honored to learn valuable insights from their caregiving journeys.

As distinctive as our caregiving journeys are, we each provide care with a profound sense of responsibility, love, compassion, and duty. The rewards of caregiving are immeasurable, and the stress is immense.

Like so many other informal caregivers, I, too, have experienced the rewards of caregiving and the detrimental effects of caregiver stress. For over two decades and continuing, I have the honor of serving as a care partner for my spouse. The years of caregiving revealed much about my limited, unhealthy beliefs. I was out of balance, and unless I addressed these limiting beliefs I would further succumb to the slippery slope of physical disease, emotional suffocation (pushing down my feelings), and mental trauma of guilt and blame. While I do not live in a constant state of caregiver utopia, I learned that caregiving requires navigating the mental and emotional trauma that naturally comes with caregiving. It is my passion to support other caregivers in their journey.

Much of what I learned is borne out of my own despondency. I was trapped in a delusion that the ultimate form of loving is caring for others. Self-sacrifice left me fatigued, hospitalized, and empty. I was on a downward spiral mentally, emotionally, and physically. Yet, throughout my journey, my perfectionism kept pushing me forward searching for balance in caregiving and self-care.

Caregiving is very much a life of balance. Thankfully, this is so. Caregiving is not a constant state of utopic love and compassion. Neither is caregiving a constant state of self-sacrifice and self-condemnation. The stepping stones in this book reflect my inward journey. A journey of self-love and self-care enabling me to navigate the mental and emotional trauma inherent in caregiving. The more rooted I am on the stepping stones, the more grounded I am in my mental and emotional stability.

May these stepping stones touch your heart and life. May your caregiving journey be rooted and grounded in self-love and self-care. May you balance the grief and stress of caregiving with inner peace and contentment. May this book benefit you in navigating the mental and emotional trauma of caregiving and rising to a higher state of mind and well-being. That is my desire for you.

Karen S. Leeman

INTRODUCTION

Rosalyn Carter states, "There are only four kinds of people in the world. Those who have been caregivers. Those who are currently caregivers. Those who will be caregivers, and those who will need a caregiver."[1] Wherever you lie within this spectrum, this book is for you.

Specifically, as an informal caregiver, you are serving in the highest of capacities for a loved one. Whether you are serving out of love or duty, it is the greatest of honors and the greatest challenge. Certainly, caring for your loved one is an expression of love. There is joy in knowing that they are well cared for. There is awe and wonder in knowing them in a different light. Yet changes in the relationship roles, assisting with daily living needs, physical decline, emotional estrangement, and diminishing cognition take a toll on the caregiver. Your grief, stress, frustration, uncertainty, and guilt seem to overpower. Often sheer responsibility calls while your mental and emotional well-being are repressed.

Each of us has a unique journey. Yet, I believe that in our uniqueness we share commonalities. So, in some sense we share in our plights. At least it brings a sense of comfort to me knowing that I am not alone in my silent suffering. I am walking this caregiver journey with you. While my caregiver experience and the disease of my loved one may differ from yours, we can learn from one another.

The stepping stones in this book are born largely out of my own experiences as a caregiver and an individual being. My beliefs and responsibilities as a caregiver nearly suffocated me mentally, emotionally, and spiritually. I knew there had to be a better way to caregive while also caring for myself. My personal journey ignited a passion within me for other caregivers struggling with the mental and emotional trauma of caregiving. And so, this book of stepping stones for caregivers became a reality.

These stepping stones are not intended to be or to replace professional services. Nor are these stepping stones meant to remove the negative aspects of caregiving. No, such negative experiences and emotions are an ever-present force in caregiving. But their presence need not dominate you. The stepping stones are like firm ground on which to stand. While the waves beat, the stepping stones are a place of safety. Dwell there more often than in the storms and quicksand of life.

Thank you for allowing me to share my journey of caregiving. You have my highest regard for endeavoring on this amazing, treacherous caregiving journey. It is my hope that the stepping stones in this book provide hope in navigating the mental and emotional trauma of caregiving and that you emerge balanced, confident, and resilient. Let not despair deter you. Return often to the stepping stones. Before long you will walk the rough terrain of caregiving with vigor. Always know in your soul that you are heroic. Caring for another is an act of unheralded bravery. You are a difference maker.

*"Much more surprising things can happen
to anyone who, when a disagreeable
or discouraged thought comes into his
mind, just has the sense to remember in
time and push it out by putting in an
agreeable, determinedly courageous one.
Two things cannot be in one place."*
—FRANCES HODGSON BURNETT, <u>THE SECRET GARDEN</u>[2]

STEPPING STONE ONE

Thought

THINKING IS A powerful force of energy, perhaps the most powerful force. If you get nothing else out of this book, gain the understanding that your thoughts are in your control. No one makes you think a thought.

On average, individuals have 6,000 thoughts every day. Some experts say that number is much higher, ranging from 12,000 – 60,000 thoughts per day. More importantly, of the average number of daily thoughts, experts say that 80 percent of those thoughts are negative, and 95 percent of thoughts are repetitive. The point is, there are many thoughts firing every day. Many of these thoughts float by unnoticed; some are held onto. Here is a typical scenario:

> *Look at the sunrise! Isn't it beautiful!...Oh, did I defrost meat for supper tonight?...I did not sleep well last night. I am definitely getting a large coffee this morning!...Oh, yes, I need to reschedule my dental appointment...Hey, I messaged my friend two days ago and have not heard anything. She must be mad at me because I did not comment on her post. Well, she can just be mad. I cannot be there for everyone. Why can't she understand that?*

Do you see what happened? Thoughts float by seemingly unnoticed in a constant stream. Many thoughts simply pass by. Some are captured, and more thoughts, emotions, and perceptions are added to the original thought. Caregiving accentuates the tendency of the mind to focus on the negative and constantly repeat the made-up story. Stories like – I cannot do this anymore! If my loved one explodes one more time, I am finished! The grief is too overwhelming! No one understands what I am going through!

What if there was a way to retrain the mind. To control the repetitive, negative thoughts. To lessen their impact. It might sound silly, woo-woo, or rubbish; but the alternative is to be caught in the repetitive cycle of negativity. Joseph Murphy says, "Never finish a negative statement; reverse it immediately, and wonders will happen in your life."[3] And that is the challenging simplicity. It takes intentional effort to stop or reverse the negative thought.

When-Then Syndrome. Why is it so difficult to stop negative thoughts and reverse their devasting impact? I believe the when-then syndrome contributes to this challenge. The when-then syndrome is a belief pattern that says when circumstances change, then I will change my thinking. This is particularly challenging for caregivers. Bombarded by emotional outbursts, physical constraints, co-dependency, and relational disconnect to name a few, caregivers face an onslaught of suffering. You push down the pain. You tell yourself such negative, hurtful stories of not being loved, not being good enough. The cycle continues until you decide to take control of your thoughts viewing your suffering in a different light.

Victor Frankl, an Australian psychiatrist and Holocaust survivor, believed that suffering is one way of finding meaning in life. Frankl penned these words:

> *"We must never forget that we may also find meaning in life even when confronted with a hopeless situation, when facing a fate that cannot be changed. For what then matters is to bear witness to the uniquely human potential at its best, which is to transform a personal tragedy into a triumph, to turn one's predicament into a human achievement. When we are no longer able to change a situation . . . we are challenged to change ourselves."*[4]

Accept Limitations. It seems contrary, but accepting the limitations of your loved one creates freedom. Acceptance is not giving up. Acceptance is not denial. Acceptance is recognition, acknowledgement that from this moment on life is in a constant state of change. If you let it, acceptance brings personal change.

Particularly in my adult years, I unknowingly sought love from the validation of others. So, when my loved one's disease progressed and emotional disconnect increased, I was devastated. Without validation, I did not feel loved. This feeling became thoughts – deep, depressive thoughts. These thoughts spiraled out of control spreading tentacles into other life relationships. Thankfully, through reflection and the teachings of renown thought leaders, I turned course. I learned that I am not what others think of me. I am a unique creation with gifts and talents to give to the world. And so are you.

Acceptance of the disease limitations of our loved ones frees caregivers to confront their own limited thinking. Are you dealing with emotional detachment, physical inability, cognitive impairment, anger outbursts? Grieve these losses and allow them to be the impetus for your personal growth. You will experience a greater depth of freedom and thought control than previously known.

Embrace Dichotomy. Negative thoughts are a normal part of caregiving. Even though negative thoughts are a typical response to stress, studies show that caregivers chide themselves with guilt over thoughts such as:

> *I have no life of my own.*
> *I cannot continue to do this.*
> *I wish this were over.*
> *I just want to run away.*

Conversely, caregivers also express an enormous sense of fulfillment from caregiving. There is joy in caring for a loved one. It brings a sense of fulfillment to give back particularly to someone who once cared for you. There is satisfaction in caregiving and knowing that your loved one is receiving excellent care.

Often these negative and positive thoughts conflict with one another. This vicious cycle of apparent dichotomous negative and positive leads to increased stress, disease, and burnout. Rather than trying to negate negative thinking (quite impossible), learn to rephrase negative and positive thoughts connecting them with the word "and" rather than "but" as in these phrases from Healthy Holistic Living.

*You are resilient **and** need a break.*
*You gave your all **and** need to back out.*
*You are independent **and** still need others.*
*You were unsure **and** things changed.*
*You are kind **and** have boundaries.*
*Others have it worse **and** your pain is valid.*
*You did your best **and** now you know more.*[5]

Change the vernacular of the mind. In the world of caregiving, it is one aspect within your control. Use the powerful force of thought to your good.

"I am no bird; and no net ensnares me: I am a free human being with an independent will."
—CHARLOTTE BRONTË, JANE EYRE[6]

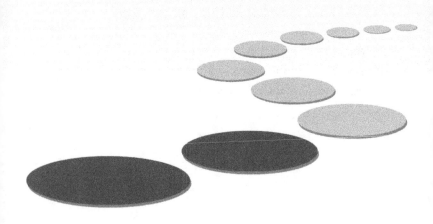

STEPPING STONE TWO

. . . .

Identity

IT IS EASY to get caught up in caregiving responsibilities and begin to define ourselves as a caregiver. At least that is what happened to me. I became engulfed in caregiving and lost the true essence of my inner being, my soul.

My Story. One day I was a wife. And then one day I was a caregiver for my spouse. It is a strange phenomenon. No one prepares you for this dichotomy. It is a synonymous symphony of love and disdain, joy and grief, my silent pain comforting another's verbal pain. For years I danced the dance. You know – keeping peace. The constant push and pull of helping, assisting, caring, while respecting independence and self-reliance. Over a decade of this crazy dance took a toll on me. I was inwardly collapsing under the weight of cognitive decline, expressive outbursts, uncontrolled anger, and emotional estrangement. Plus, life has its own challenges outside of caregiving. So, I also carried the burden of financial instability, the blame for family fracture, the shame of other's life choices, and the responsibility of caregiving for aging parents. Eventually the inner turmoil led me on an inward journey of realizing that love for myself was the missing element. Not that I was inflicting physical harm on myself or suicidal. My thoughts, however, were out of balance. Serving others became by identity. I believed that serving others was synonymous with loving myself. My self-talk was negative and self-condemning. Loving myself, changing my thought patterns and self-talk is my steppingstone for inner peace. It is my inward sanctuary from which I draw strength, stamina, flexibility, and perseverance while caregiving. Self-love is knowing that I am valuable. I am significant. I matter.

What keeps you from realizing your identity? Here are three self-limiting statements that you can rephrase into empowering beliefs for yourself.

I am Powerless. Yes, caregiving is rewarding; and it is daunting. You are often paralyzed with powerlessness. You cannot make your loved one whole. You cannot reason with your loved one. You cannot restore your relationship to what it once was. This overwhelming sense of powerlessness begins to invade your thoughts to where you believe that you are powerless. Do you see the subtle shift? Sure, you are limited in what you can do for your loved one; but you are a powerful being with unlimited potential. This is true regardless of your present or past circumstances. You give care. Caregiving does not define your identity. You are a unique, gifted individual. Shift your thoughts from I am powerless to I matter. Say this to yourself internally and aloud. Say it repeatedly every day. You will see the difference because you matter.

I am Unlovable. Is it any wonder that caregivers often feel unlovable? You engage in personal caregiving tasks that often leave you feeling embarrassed or uneasy. You are bored and isolated. You feel verbally traumatized even though you know it is the disease. The paradox of caregiving while juggling multiple roles takes a toll on you until you begin to feel unlovable. For me, the knowledge that these experiences are a normal part of the disease process just does not equate to feeling lovable. You must be comfortable with yourself apart from your loved one. Remember, it is not caregiving that makes you loveable. You already are a lovable individual. Change your self-talk from "I am unlovable" to "I am valuable". Not because of what you do, but because of who you are. Believe it to be true because it is.

I am Unworthy. What a defeating statement. You might feel unworthy in your caregiver role. No wonder. Most caregivers have little to no training. Maybe caregiving is not your forte. Feeling guilty, you compensate with anger and frustration, exacerbating the feeling of unworthiness. Or you might generally feel unworthy. Maybe life choices or family dynamics negatively impacted you. You view life through the lens of past circumstances reliving those experiences in multiple ways. You are not your past. You are not your experiences. You are significant. Change your mindset from I am unworthy to I am significant. You are worthy. You make a difference just by being yourself.

You are a unique individual designed for a unique purpose. Though engaged in the high calling of caregiving, your worth exists prior to caregiving, during caregiving, and subsequent to caregiving. Undefined by your caregiving role, You matter, You are valued, You are significant.

"All great spirituality is about what we do with our pain. If we do not transform our pain, we will transmit it to those around us."
—RICHARD ROHR[7]

STEPPING STONE THREE

. . . .

Release

EMOTIONAL BAGGAGE. WE all carry it. You know what I am talking about. Someone said something to you in grade school, and now you are self-conscious about your appearance. Kids made fun of you, so you became withdrawn. Your parents did not have a lot of money, so wealth is not achievable for you. One parent was hard on you; the other was passive. Now you are insecure and overcompensate. The emotional baggage sneaks up on you. Before you know it, you are carrying around heavy weights of shame, blame, guilt, distrust, resentment, and regret to name a few. This emotional baggage is then manifested in fear, worry, doubt, anger, depression, and stagnation. It weighs you down undermining your potential. You plod along through life often not recognizing your emotional baggage or its effects.

In his book, *Help Yourself. Celebrating the Rewards of Resilience and Gratitude,* Dave Pelzer writes from his heart and personal experience on the subject of freeing oneself from life experiences and the meaning we give to them. Concerning the power of releasing unresolved issues, Mr. Pelzer writes:

> Everyone of us has a past. All of us have had
> our share of problems. No one has a perfect

> life. Loved ones pass away. Parents divorce.
> Others don't strive as hard and don't deserve
> the prized promotion receive it.[8]

Mr. Pelzer goes on to expound on the impact of unresolved issues. He says: "The single most critical element I have found that prevents individuals from achieving their greatness is unresolved issues. It doesn't matter who you are – CEO, single parent, teen, a celebrity, or any other everyday folk - you can never reach your full potential unless you deal with and rid yourself of whatever may be troubling you."[9]

Caregiving adds another dimension to this phenomenon, exaggerating our rehearsed response. Your loved one yells at you and has outbursts of anger. You take it personally and respond in like kind or in self-condemnation. Your loved one is distant and you feel unlovable convincing yourself of a self-made reality. The difference for caregivers is that our reactive response is more potent, damaging, and has an increased negative span of effect.

What should we do with this emotional baggage that is not serving us well? How do we stop the cycle and avoid the "land mines" of emotional baggage reactivity? Take advice from Brigitte Nicole. "One of the most courageous decisions you'll ever make is to finally let go of what is hurting your heart and soul."[10] Empty the suitcase! Release the emotional baggage! Let it go!

Release is a profoundly powerful action to remove emotional baggage. But exactly how do you release emotional baggage? Before we discuss the three suggestions below, let me interject a caveat. Certainly, some situations require professional intervention. Seek professional help as necessary. This content is aimed at common life challenges that are mishandled and build into a mountainous emotional barrier. Also, this content is aimed for the caregiver – addressing your emotional baggage. We cannot correct the emotional baggage of our loved one. This might seem contrary. After all, isn't this the point? Isn't it by our loved one changing that we finally experience peace and contentment? The truth is – that is not the pathway because you will experience another similar event that will once again trigger your emotional baggage response. So, release your emotional baggage!

Understand Your Perception. You start your life journey fully equipped, free of emotional baggage. As you begin to experience life, make choices, and respond to life events, you pack unresolved issues into your emotional baggage. Often the weight of the baggage is not noticeable until your adult life. By then, you have overstuffed your emotional baggage causing it to spill out on yourself and others leaving a trail of impactful damage.

How does this happen? Thoughts create feelings. Feelings create attitude. Attitudes create belief. And belief creates perception. It is through your perception of life events that you began to absorb emotional baggage distorting your whole, perfectly created beings.

Change Your Mental Dialogue. While caregiving we experience heightened, emotional responses. Our loved

13

one requires an increasing amount of physical, mental, and emotional care. We feel isolation, depression, and resentment. Our mental dialogue lingers on phrases of pity, insecurity, inadequacy, anger, frustration, and irritation. On and on goes the mental dialogue. Everyday. All the time creating a mental and emotional reality based on your perception. I do the same. We all do it.

What if you change your mental dialogue? How does that diffuse the situation? It certainly does not stop the disease spilling out of your loved one. It does change your perception and, hence, your response. Change your mental dialogue from one of negativity to acknowledging that your loved one does or says what they know at the time. Rather than ruminating, choose uplifting phrases that acknowledge your value.

Tell yourself a different story. Ruminating – dwelling on negative thoughts and feelings – leads to further distress. And worse, ruminating inevitably leads to the second arrow. What is the second arrow? The second arrow is the meaning that you give to the first arrow or offense. It is your reaction and emotional response. It is more painful than the first arrow. The first arrow is often out of your control while the second arrow is within your control. For example, your loved one snaps angrily at you when you were merely trying to help. This is the first arrow. It is painful. You respond emotionally by snapping back or by internalizing – I cannot do anything right. This is the second arrow. It brings more pain but is in your control. Acknowledge the pain and recognize your choice to respond externally and internally. It is not about never experiencing pain. You do have the power to minimize the second arrow of pain. Each time you choose not to shoot the second arrow, you free yourself.

Paul Coelho offers this perspective: "Let things go. Release them. Detach yourself from them. Stop turning on your emotional television to watch the same program over and over again, the one that shows how much you suffered from a certain loss: that is only poisoning you, nothing else."[11] Are you ready to release the emotional baggage that is weighing you down? Are you willing to change your perception, your mental dialogue, and your story? Walk down a different street. You will find sweet release!

*"Self-compassion is simply giving
the same kindness to ourselves that
we would give to others."*
—CHRISTOPHER GERMER[12]

STEPPING STONE FOUR

· ·

Self-Compassion

SELF-COMPASSION IS CRITICAL for caregivers, for without it we are left to our own detrimental judgment. Self-compassion is the kindness we show to ourselves. It is allowing ourselves to feel our emotions without self-condemnation. Somehow caregivers seem to believe the unrealistic notion that embracing our emotions is weakness. That we must constantly be strong. Unwavering. In reality, properly embracing our emotions to move forward with renewed vigor minimizes caregiver burnout.

Certainly, caring for others challenges us to our core. It is this very act of questioning and wavering that beckons self-compassion. Self-compassion allows us to feel our emotions, express self-kindness, and experience the most glorious personal transformation. As Peggi Spears writes, "Most of all, I learned more about me – how I react in time of crisis, how long I can endure, what I can withstand and no longer withstand, how my body and emotions are connected, and how they respond to stress. I discovered that my health matters. My life matters. I matter!"[13]

There are many benefits to embracing self-compassion including reduced stress, mental clarity, emotional well-being, and physical strength. Self-compassion softens the mistakes we inevitably make as caregivers. It is also the link to lessen our internal response to the emotional strain of caregiving. Self-compassion is a viable coping mechanism to release our tension from the constant barrage of verbal and emotional onslaughts. Self-compassion is our fuel that re-energizes you on your caregiving journey.

Accept. One of the most profound, releasing, and extremely difficult aspects of caregiving is to accept the decline in your loved one due to disease. I can sense your rebuttal - I am not giving up! My loved one is not that bad. Acceptance of decline is not giving up. It is acknowledging that life is different than it used to be. There are limitations that were not previously present. Conversations that once were, are no more.

When my loved one's emotional disengagement began to heighten, I was devastated to say the least. Words escape me to convey the depth of despair I experienced. After months of condemning introspection, disdain for my body, and intense sadness I began to accept the emotional disengagement as an impersonal disease process. I still miss the emotional connection, but I no longer expect it. This shift in thinking was the key for me to connect on a different level, to move forward in adaptation, and to experience personal peace. Ruth Fischel eloquently expresses acceptance as "It is a beautiful experience being with ourselves at a level of complete acceptance. When that begins to happen, when you give up resistance and needing to be perfect, a peace will come over you as you have never known."[14]

Acknowledge. Self-compassion is not the absence of emotion nor is it repressing emotion. Let's face it. Caregiving is a rewarding, emotional roller coaster. We experience love, grief, joy, sadness, happiness, anger, frustration, doubt, fear – a whole gambit of emotions on a continuous cycle. Kristin Neff points out that "painful feelings are, by their very nature, temporary. They will weaken over time as long as we don't prolong or amplify them through resistance or avoidance. The only way to eventually free ourselves from debilitating pain, therefore, is to be with it as it is. The only way out is through."[15] Ignoring these feelings, minimizing their presence, or pushing them down inside only serves to weaken you physically, mentally, and emotionally. Acknowledge that it is appropriate to experience grief, anger, fear, and frustration. Acknowledge that all your emotions – positive and negative – are valid. Let yourself appropriately release these emotions. In so doing, you will be free.

Alleviate. Emotions need release in a healthy manner. Without release, emotions build up over time and eventually spill out, leaving a trail of destruction. Have a good cry. Scream into a pillow. Talk to a friend. Go for a nature walk. Try deep breathing exercises. Talk yourself down. Repeat a positive mantra. Give yoga a try. Join a support group. Find an outlet. Be compassionate to yourself. Give yourself permission to alleviate stress. In so doing, you are a better person and caregiver. Be mindful of the words of Kristin Neff. "This is a moment of suffering. Suffering is part of life. May I be kind to myself in this moment. May I give myself the compassion I need."[16]

Aspire. Selfcare begins with self-compassion. Give yourself permission to be compassionate toward yourself. Among your various responsibilities, self-compassion lags toward the bottom of the list. Caregivers strive to give the best care to their loved one. They often short circuit their own health and mental and emotional well-being. Long days and sleepless nights are the norm. And commonly, caregivers experience guilt over a minute amount of self-compassion.

<u>Practice self-forgiveness.</u> Oh, the overwhelming guilt! There seems to be no shortage. We guilt ourselves feeling that our care for our loved one is somehow inadequate. We feel guilty about our relationships because our time is overly stretched between responsibilities. Guilt overshadows rare moments of laughter with friends. Go easy on yourself. After all, you are a human being, a unique individual. You need and deserve compassionate self-forgiveness. Sure, caregivers make mistakes. We lose our temper. We become fatigued. We are human. Accept your humanity, forgive yourself, and move forward.

<u>Practice self-kindness.</u> Do you find your self-talk to be negative, self-condemning? Are you extremely hard on yourself? Give yourself some slack. Change your vernacular. Use words of kindness and appreciation toward yourself. You carry a heavy load. Treat yourself well. Aspire toward self-compassion.

Bob Marley and the Wailers released "Three Little Birds" as a single in 1980. Better known as "Every Little Thing is Gonna be Alright," this beloved song with its catchy tune is a reminder of the futility of worry. Accept, acknowledge, and alleviate your emotions knowing that everything works out for your good.

Don't <u>worry</u> 'bout a thing
'Cause <u>every</u> little <u>thing</u> gonna be alright
Singing' don't <u>worry</u> about a thing
'Cause <u>every</u> little <u>thing</u> gonna be alright[17]

Go easy on yourself. Show yourself some kindness. We are doing this thing called caregiving in kind of a free fall style. Give yourself some room. Accept. Acknowledge. Alleviate.

*"Learning to distance yourself from
all the negativity is one of the greatest
lessons to achieve inner peace."*
—ROY T. BENNETT, <u>THE LIGHT IN THE HEART</u>[18]

STEPPING STONE FIVE

Peace

CAREGIVING AFFORDS JOYOUS rewards. There is the sheer satisfaction of caring for someone you love. The knowledge that they are being cared for with utmost respect and well-being. There is opportunity to know your loved one in a different way. And there is ample opportunity for personal growth.

As joyous as caregiving is, it also has unlimited stressors. There are empty promises of help and support. Well-meaning family and friends voice their opinions about your caregiving. Your loved one's needs are not apparent to the public creating internal conflict and confusion. You are faced with the quagmire of the medical system. And, most importantly, we all tend to carry our own negative perceptions.

The words of the great hymn, "It is Well with My Soul," penned by Horatio Spafford, are a lovely illustration of peace during tribulations. His life story serves as an anchor of hope.

A successful lawyer and businessman, Horatio Spafford lived in Chicago in the late 19th century. Though a successful and religious individual, he did not escape tragedy and loss. The Great Chicago Fire of 1871 destroyed much of his real estate holdings. Shortly thereafter, his only son died. Inspite of these tragic losses, Spafford remained steadfast to his faith and dedicated to helping other individuals.

In 1873, Spafford's wife and four daughters boarded the Ville du Havre bound for Europe for a family vacation. However, in the middle of the Atlantic Ocean, the Ville du Havre collided with another ship. The death toll of this tragic incident was 226 passengers including Spafford's four daughters.

Spafford, upon receiving the news, immediately traveled to Europe to be with his grieving wife. During his journey, Spafford wrote a poem that later was set to music known as "It is Well with My Soul", one of the most beloved hymns of time.

> *When peace like a river, attendeth my way,*
> *When sorrows like sea billows roll—*
> *Whatever my lot, thou hast taught me to say*
> *It is well, it is well with my soul.*[19]

The multiple tragedies faced by Spafford are a beautiful reminder to find purpose and meaning in the midst of loss and negativity. Not to minimize the tragedies experienced by Spafford, caregiving also offers us opportunities to rise above the negativity.

Make Peace with Yourself. I did not realize it at the time, but people pleasing became a way of life for me. More than that, pleasing others was a noble way of showing love for God and for other people. As caregiving mounted, career demands increased, and family life faltered, I began sinking into the self-destructive clutches of shame, blame, and guilt. These low energy, disease forming emotions took a toll until I began the process to make peace with myself. I am more balanced now most of the time. I understand that I have value. I matter. I am significant. I love myself and serve others within the boundary of self-respect rather than serving others to obtain my value.

Why share this and what does that have to do with caregiving? Well, I think that being out of balance in our beliefs is common and becomes heightened with caregiving. Take this people pleasing mentality for self-worth and mix in emotional detachment from the loved one that you are caring for and you have a recipe for disaster. Being rooted in your own value, making peace with yourself, provides a firm foundation to manage the roller coaster experience of caregiving.

<u>Believe in your own value.</u> You are perfect and whole, a unique creation with unlimited potential. Believe that. Say wholesome statements to yourself. Love yourself then serve others rather than serving others to love yourself.

<u>Raise your emotional value.</u> Every emotion has a vibrational frequency – high or low, fast or slow. The emotion of shame, for example, has the lowest emotional vibrational frequency and weakens the body. Gratitude has a vibrational frequency as that of love and strengthens the body. The more time you spend in gratitude, the healthier will be your body and spirit and the greater agility you possess for caregiver stressors.

True are the words of Dalai Lama XIV. "We can never obtain peace in the outer world until we make peace with ourselves."[20]

Make Peace with Others. Family members and friends are sometimes helpful and well-intended. Even well-meaning intentions, though, can be perceived as annoying or insensitive. Or you may experience intentional rudeness and insensitivity. You may be the recipient of unfulfilled promised help. Whatever the case, these situations can fester and create resentment. While it might feel right, even good for a while, resentment acts as a binding agent. It binds you like a tether to the person or situation making you a prisoner. Forgiveness – making peace with others – is the key to unlock the prison of resentment.

Forgiveness is not condoning. Forgiveness is not acceptance. It is not looking the other way or ignoring the situation. Forgiveness is release from resentment. It is personal freedom. And most importantly, forgiveness sets boundaries and expectations.

Forgiveness is freedom. Andy Puddicombe, Headspace co-founder, says, "We can't always change what's happening around us, but we can change what happens within us."[21] Forgiving or making peace with others is a personal, inward experience. It does not necessarily mean that the other person acknowledges or asks for forgiveness. Making peace with others and establishing your personal boundaries frees you from guilt and blame allowing you to function unhindered as an individual and as a caregiver.

Make Peace With the Past. You are not what other people say. Your past does not define you but rather empowers self-reliance. We often are caught in a vicious, repetitive cycle of the past. I am not good enough. I do not deserve wealth. Nothing good ever happens to me. These statements only perpetuate that very reality, so make peace with the past.

Accept the past. People do what they know to do. It is the best that they know at the time. It is not excusing or condoning the actions of the past, but rather changing the perception of the past and giving it new meaning. Accept the past, learn from the past, and paint yourself a new reality.

Focus on the present. Rather than living in the wake of the past or the worry of the future, enjoy the present moments. How can that happen with all the life and caregiving stressors? It takes fortitude and persistence – qualities you possess. Louise Hay has a saying that I often use to settle my mind and focus on the present: "I am well. Everything is working out for my highest good. Out of this situation will come only good. I am safe."

"Some tension", according to Joan Borysenki, "is necessary for the soul to grow, and we can put that tension to good use. We can look for every opportunity to give and receive love, to appreciate nature, to heal our wounds and the wounds of others, to forgive, and to serve."[22] Stress is imminent in caregiving. Rather than responding to stress with stress, eliminate its effects by creating space in your life for peace.

"The miracle of gratitude is that it shifts your perception to such an extent that it changes the world you see."
—Dr. Rober Holden[23]

STEPPING STONE SIX

. . . .

Gratitude

MELODY BEATTIE shares a poignant thought on gratitude.

> *Gratitude unlocks the fullness of life. It turns*
> *what we have into enough, and more. It*
> *turns denial into acceptance, chaos to order,*
> *confusion to clarity. It can turn a meal into*
> *a feast, a house into a home, a stranger into*
> *a friend. It turns problems into gifts, failures*
> *into successes, the unexpected into perfect*
> *timing, and mistakes into important events.*
> *It can turn an existence into a real life, and*
> *disconnected situations into important and*
> *beneficial lessons. Gratitude makes sense of*
> *our past, brings peace for today, and creates*
> *a vision for tomorrow.*[24]

In your caregiving role, your life is often a constant wave of change. Like walking a balance beam, you impose on a treacherous journey of keeping peace, maintaining a sense of consistency, and overextending yourself. The beauty of life and its seasonal changes are unnoticed due to over exertion, fatigue, and the loss of our inner essence.

Gratitude is excellent for stress reduction. It does not

require any tools, specific location, or specified time. It can be practiced anytime, anywhere. Gratitude improves your mental well-being, boosts your immune system, and improves sleep resulting in healthier relationships and self-happiness. It is said that gratitude has a vibrational frequency higher than that of love.

Gratitude is Rephrasing Your Inner Dialogue. Gratitude is not the absence of challenges or negativity. It is seeing life – joys and challenges, positive experiences and negative experiences – through the lens of gratitude. It is knowing that everything which comes into your life serves a purpose for your greater good. Gratitude goes against the grain when your loved one is suffering, losing ability, or becoming unrecognizable. I am not suggesting that you express gratitude for the incurable disease of your loved one; rather rephrase your inner dialogue from limiting phrases to powerful, uplifting phrases.

Gratitude is Redirecting Your Thoughts. Sometimes life is hard. As a caregiver, I know it is. Caregivers face the same battle every day. Gratitude is downright challenging. You will not know its reward, though, if you do not start. So, begin with short phrases. I am grateful for this day. I am grateful for sunshine. Then move on. Learn to incorporate the feeling of gratitude. The combination of words and feelings when practiced regularly over time redirects your thoughts shortening the cycle of negativity and lengthening the cycle of gratitude.

Gratitude is a Life Practice. Gratitude is meant to be lived daily. Yes, when life is going well. And, yes, when life is going poorly. When life is going well, it is easy to become complacent. No need for gratitude, right? Everything is going smoothly. Wrong! And when life is going poorly – well, who wants to be grateful then? You see, gratitude does not view life by these two spectrums. Gratitude rises above the good, the bad, the joys, the challenges. For as surely as spring follows winter and summer turns into fall a life grounded in gratitude understands that life experiences mimic the seasonal flows. Gratitude is the thread that binds together sorrow and joy, peace and discomfort, hope and hopelessness.

To start your journey of gratitude, use the gratitude statements below and see the life difference it makes.

- I am grateful for the mental and emotional capacity to rise above life's challenges.
- I am grateful for my peace of mind.
- I am grateful for laughter.
- I am grateful for the freedom to choose my own thoughts.
- I am grateful for this day and the endless opportunities it offers.
- I am grateful for the cyclical change of seasons for it is a reminder of the natural flow of life.
- I am grateful for family and friends and acknowledge where they are at this moment in life.
- I am grateful for the ability to reason and discern.
- I am grateful for the control I have over my thoughts and feelings.
- I am grateful for the gift of life.
- I am grateful for moments of reflection.

- I am grateful for the gift of time.
- I am grateful for intuition.
- I am grateful for each new day.
- I am grateful for my inner and outer beauty.
- I am grateful for quiet moments of solitude.
- I am grateful for leisure time with friends.
- I am grateful for time with my loved one.
- I am grateful for resilience.
- I am grateful for the painful joy of loving and being loved so deeply.
- I am grateful for the beautiful sunrise and gorgeous sunset as a reminder of daily consistency.
- I am grateful for poise during challenging times.
- I am grateful for courage to face the unknown.
- I am grateful for strength to meet the daily challenges.
- I am grateful for times to refresh and reset.
- I am grateful for adaptability to the ever-changing needs of my loved one.
- I am grateful for soulful pondering.
- I am grateful for choosing to take time for myself.
- I am grateful for restorative practices that improve my mind, body, and spirit.
- I am grateful for forgiveness toward myself and others.
- I am grateful for the ability to release mental, physical, and emotional anguish and to replenish my spirit.

Gratitude encompasses all that comes into our life whether we perceive it as joyous or despairing. Gratitude changes our perception. As Alphonse Karr wrote, "We can complain because rose bushes have thorns, or rejoice because thorns have roses."[25] Let gratitude stabilize you on the wave of change.

To everything turn, turn, turn
There is a season turn, turn, turn
And a time to every purpose under Heaven
A time to be born, a time to die
A time to plant, a time to reap
A time to kill, a time to heal
A time to laugh, a time to weep[26]

STEPPING STONE SEVEN

Flow

PETE SEEGER, IN his 1965 hit folk song, "Turn, Turn, Turn" performed by the Byrds, beautifully expresses the natural flow of life. The lyrics suggest the reality of an everchanging, turning world in which there is a time and a place for everything.

You, in your caregiving role, experience daily an everchanging reality often not knowing what to expect from one minute to the next. Your life is an emotional roller coaster of joy, love, and hope coupled with stress, frustration, and despair. Just when life is going well, financial instability, mental and emotional trauma, depression, and fatigue overwhelm you. After enjoying time with family and friends, you feel a sense of guilt and loneliness. Life is a constant mental, emotional, and physical wave in which you are tossed about leaving marks of insecurity, fear, and inadequacy.

You can find your footing. You can learn to ride the wave with these three practices.

Look to Nature. Embrace the harmonious, cyclical rhythm of nature. Regardless of external circumstances, spring follows winter, and turns into summer. Summer then welcomes the beauty of autumn. And autumn gives way to winter. So, the cycle continues. Unhindered. Unhampered. And so it is with you. Like spring, you have seasons of growth. There is newness and beauty. Perhaps a child or grandchild is birthed. Maybe you experience personal growth, fresh insight. The warmth of summer invites a sense of joy and brightness. Perhaps you experience happiness in an accomplishment and bask in the fragrance of life if but for a moment. And then comes autumn. A season of beauty, truth, and reflection. And winter in its stillness is a time for solitude and inner reflection.

This does not mean that in summer you are happy and carefree while in winter you are lonely and solitary. Rather this mental, emotional, and physical cycle occurs in a rhythmic pattern. Learn to embrace it. Each cycle has a purpose and transformational power. Yes, welcome grief and loneliness for the lessons they teach. Then move quickly out of that cycle into a cycle of love and peace. You have more control over the length of the cycles than what you might realize. The goal is not to remove the unpleasantness of the cycles but to embrace them as a vital component of your life. They are there to serve a purpose.

Accept Grief. Grief is a normal aspect of caregiving. The normalcy of grief does not minimize it but rather brings it to the forefront. Western culture lacks in recognition of grief. Lose a parent, and if you are working outside the home in your caregiving role, you might get five days of paid bereavement. Five days. Grief is not over in five days. In fact, while you are caregiving, grief is pretty much an everyday experience. Specifically, these two types of caregiving grief are virtually not recognized.

<u>Ambiguous grief.</u> Ambiguous grief in caregiving is the sense of losing a loved one who is still living. It is grieving the loss of physical ability, cognition, emotional connection, or mental capacity of your loved one. It is the recognition that your loved one is no longer the same person in full or in part. While ambiguous grief is on-going and lacking closure, it serves to demonstrate the immense love you experience with your loved one. A love of this nature is a precious, immeasurable force. Cry. Allow yourself to feel the pain. Be kind to yourself. Cycle yourself back to a state of love and laughter.

<u>Hidden grief.</u> Similar to ambiguous grief, hidden grief happens when you recognize changes in your loved one, but these changes are not recognized by the outside world. For example, you see behavior that is outside of your loved one's norm, but to the outside world your loved one appears normal. Your loved one may look and act normal. Your loved one may convince medical professionals that they are fine. But what you see and experience daily paints a different picture. The reality of your experience versus the lack of external validation, sets the stage for questioning yourself. Hidden grief may even lead you to change your perception of reality in agreement with your loved one and external validation. Know that you are not alone in this dilemma. Many caregivers experience hidden grief. Stand strong in your convictions. Take time to replenish and rejuvenate your own well-being.

Embrace Challenges. Every caregiver faces challenges. It is innate in the cyclical flow of life. It is what you do with challenges, how you respond to challenges that serves to either refine you or define you. Your loved one lashes out in anger. You respond in like kind. This creates more anger. Or your loved one behaves irrationally. You respond irrationally or mockingly. There is a life principle that like creates like. So much of your caregiving life is out of your control. How you respond to challenges is within your control. Set boundaries. Forgive yourself. Designate a quiet place for yourself. Practice mindfulness.

Learn the Art of Non-resistance. Do you ever have days where everything seemingly goes wrong? You get every red light. Spill coffee on your clothes. The more you try to clean it, the worse it gets. Now you are late for work and are then given an impossible deadline. And that does not even touch all that happened prior between you and your loved one – high demands, the exchange of words, and the never-ending cycle of thoughts. You just want to be in control. Get through a day without problems or controversy. Often we view these experiences as unpleasant, maybe even painful. We squirm in vain casting blame and disappointment. The art of non-resistance welcomes these experiences because they are refining tools that develop wisdom, patience, maturity, and inner well-being.

Resistance to change or asserting control of events leads to struggle. Rather than resisting, learn the art of non-resistance. Learn to embrace change, hardship, and negative feelings. They are your teachers. Learn to accept them with compassion as tools for your growth. Allow the natural flow of life, with all its uncertainties, to be opportunities for strength and stamina.

Navigate the seasons of caregiving knowing that each season serves a purpose. Celebrate the natural flow of caregiving knowing that everything that happens to you serves a purpose for your highest good.

"Within you, there is a stillness and a sanctuary to which you can retreat at any time and be yourself."
—Hermann Hesse[27]

STEPPING STONE EIGHT

Stillness

DO YOU FEEL the push and pull - needs of your loved one, family needs, job pressures, financial woes, opinions of others, medical concerns, physical strain, responsibility upon responsibility? The strain is constant. Despite the joy of caregiving, it is no wonder that caregivers are at risk for disease, depression, and decline in mental and emotional health. To combat these effects, research indicates the value for caregivers to have adequate sleep, exercise regularly, eat a healthy diet, and maintain meaningful relationships. I wholeheartedly agree and advocate the prerequisite of regularly quieting the mind. Rooting the mind in stillness and being grounded in self-love enables sleep, exercise, nutrition, and friendship to initiate from the heart rather than from a sense of duty or even guilt.

Our thoughts are merely thoughts cycling by like dandelions floating in the air. Which ones you grab onto and how you perceive them is your choice. Dr. Joe Dispenza says, "Your thoughts are incredibly powerful. Choose yours wisely."[28] Apart from controlling thoughts – not the absence of thought but choosing which ones to allow into the mind – thoughts will whip you about like the destruction of tornadic wind. Chronic caregiver stress weakens the body leading to burnout, a weakened immune system, and depression. Quieting the mind is the gateway to stress relief.

Mindfulness. Mindfulness is not the absence of doubt, fear, or negativity. Mindfulness is not about eliminating or controlling thoughts. Mindfulness is about stillness. It is giving space to the myriad of thoughts without judgement or criticism. It is acknowledging the present moment – not taking a present thought into the past or into the future. For example:

- I cannot take much more! I am stressed to the max! (present moment)
- My loved one cannot help it. I feel guilty for being so stressed. (assigning judgement/criticism)
- I knew caregiving was not for me. I have done such a lousy job of caregiving. (taking the present thought into the past)
- I do not have what it takes to continue caregiving. My loved one deserves better. (taking the present thought into the future)

This is a common thought scenario. The key is to recognize the thought. Avoid judging yourself for having these thoughts. It is quite natural. It is only a thought – neither positive nor negative. Just a thought. Only when meaning – judgement or criticism – is assigned to the thought, does the thought become problematic.

When the mind wanders assigning meaning to thoughts – and the mind will wander – simply recognize it and redirect the thought back to a non-judgmental state. And the beauty of this practice is that it can happen virtually anywhere, anytime. A dedicated time or space is not required for mindfulness making it accessible to caregivers.

To begin a mindfulness practice, implement these techniques:

<u>Take deep breaths.</u> Deep breathing relaxes the body and resets emotional responses reducing stress and anxiety.

<u>Utilize loving kindness.</u> Speak kindly to yourself. Give yourself a break. Realize that you are heroic and extraordinary, and you need time to reframe.

<u>Practice gratitude.</u> Gratitude is the quickest way to raise your awareness. The practice of gratitude need not be complicated. Even expressing gratitude for something simple, like the smell of coffee, shifts the mindset and opens the pathway for increased gratitude.

Remember, regularly practicing mindfulness keeps you grounded, rooted, and calm while caregiving. Sakyoung Mipham echoes this thought. She says, "The body benefits from movement, and the mind benefits from stillness."[29] Make mindfulness a part of your life.

Meditation. Meditation is a powerful practice for calmness and physical relaxation. Further, meditation reduces the feeling of loneliness and depression. Its healing properties have a therapeutic effect on the mind, attributing to increased health and reduced stress. Additional benefits of meditation include:

- Improved emotional well-being
- Stress management
- Reframed mind
- Increased creative solutions
- Reduced anxiety, sleep issues, and tension headaches

Meditation need not be a time-consuming practice. Feel free to explore the infinite techniques and practices of meditation. Meditation is life changing if you let it be. Avoid the tendency to meditate then go about your day as though you never meditated. Let the meditation sink into your thoughts and behaviors throughout the day. In this way you will fully experience the mental and emotional well-being aspects of a daily meditation practice. As Andy Puddicombe say, "We can't always change what's happening around us, but we can change what happens within us."[30] Let the practice of meditation be the impetus for a state of calmness.

Affirmations. Affirmations are simple, positive statements. Similar to mindfulness and meditation, affirmations serve to shift the mind's focus creating a healthy, wholesome environment for caregivers to lean into and to serve from. Affirmations train the mind to shift focus from negative to positive. These positive statements imbue confidence, settle the mind, establish a grounded foundation on which to perform caregiver duties, reframe perception, and create an empowering environment.

Like meditation, affirmations need not be a time-consuming practice. Write your own affirmations or explore the endless online avenues. Twenty minutes or so of affirmations in the morning, set the tone for the day. And like meditation, affirmations are not merely nice positive sayings for a warm, fuzzy feeling. They benefit little when the remainder of the day is spent ruminating on negative self-talk. Let these affirmations infuse your mind. Return to them often throughout the day. Having a rough moment? Take a break. Go to a different room or to the restroom, etc. where you can reset your well-being with positive affirmations.

To start, here are a few affirmations designed specifically for caregivers:

- I take time, without guilt, to refresh my soul, my spirit.
- I speak kindly to myself.
- I live in the moment. My past is gone and does not define me.
- I am capable of any challenges that come my way.
- My thoughts are powerful, imbuing my inner reality and creating my outer reality.

If you are still not convinced about the powerful effect of affirmations, let the words of Claud M. Briston sink in. "Repetition of the same chant, the same incantations, the same affirmations leads to belief, and once that belief becomes a deep conviction, things begin to happen."[31]

Take control of what happens within you. Give yourself the delight of stillness.

"To care for those who once cared for us is one of the highest honors."
—TIA WALKER[32]

STEPPING STONE NINE

Valor

CAREGIVERS FACE ENORMOUS challenges and often engage in grueling tasks, endure emotional strain, face mounting hardships, and experience multiple modalities of grief. And they get up and do it all over again the next day! Caregivers exemplify valor!

Merriam-Webster defines valor as strength of mind or spirit that enables a person to encounter danger with firmness; personal bravery.

While there is much emphasis on the challenges of caregiving, there are also many benefits associated with caregiving that are worthy of recognition. When you are down and out, as all caregivers are from time to time, remember your value as a caregiver. Caring for another is a great treasure of life.

- Caregivers are the backbone of the American healthcare system and represent the largest support system for loved ones.
- Caregivers provide life-changing, life-supporting care for seniors, persons with disabilities, and non-seniors with chronic or non-curable diseases

      while also maintaining full-time jobs and other responsibilities.

- Caregivers are a profoundly significant source of love, care, nourishment, and companionship to their loved one.
- Caregivers are the cornerstone of society, tending to the medical, emotional, physical, and spiritual needs of their loved one.
- Caregivers offer a hands-on, valuable role within the caregiving spectrum.

Courage. Whether or not you consider yourself as courageous, you demonstrate courage daily. Every day you muster strength from within, from your faith, to support your loved one. It is not an easy path. Often the challenges are enormous. You may face lack of support of family. You may experience dynamics from your loved one that are not visible to the public. This dichotomy wreaks havoc on your emotional and mental stability. And yet, despite the odds, you show up ready to care for your loved one. That, my friend, is the height of courage. You are a hero in your own right. You are not perfect. You doubt. You have misgivings. And you emerge through it with renewed strength and ability to face fear. Dr. Elisabeth Kubler-Ross states, "The most beautiful people we have known are those who have known defeat, known suffering, known struggle, known loss, and have found their way out of the depths. These persons have an appreciation, a sensitivity, and an understanding of life that fills them with compassion, gentleness, and a deep loving concern. Beautiful people do not just happen."[33]

When courage is faltering, as it will, think on these truths for increased vitality.

- My mistakes teach me more about myself every day.
- I have many strengths that support me through hard times.
- Laughter is a source of strength through adversity.
- I strive for progress, not perfection.
- I carry courage with me always.

Perseverance. Whether you have chosen the role of caregiver or it has chosen you, caregivers demonstrate perseverance. Throughout the typical valleys and peaks of caregiving, you steadfastly put forth the effort despite challenges and setbacks. Perseverance is not the absence of fear, difficulty, or despair. It is pressing on despite fear, difficulty, or despair.

Caregiving often calls you to repetitively perform tasks or phrases. The repetition is exhausting, often leading to fatigue and annoyance. Perseverance recognizes the normalcy of these feelings and yet presses on. Disappointments and setbacks are typical in caregiving. Your perseverance allows you to muster through.

Caregivers also deal with complex disease management issues. With little to no training, you embark on a primary caregiver role that requires expertise in fields beyond your knowledge all while maintaining a career, a home, and relationships. "A hero", as Christopher Reeve acknowledges, "is an ordinary individual who finds the strength to persevere and endure despite overwhelming obstacles."[34]. Yet even the word heroic does not fully capture the extraordinary strength and stamina of caregivers. Never underestimate yourself. You are of priceless value!

<u>Resilience.</u> Caregivers face adversity and a constantly changing landscape. Despite these challenges, caregivers confront these obstacles with resilience. Caregivers learn to uncover their capacity to withstand and quickly recover from adversity. As the caregiver journey develops, you respond with adaptability. Honoring your relationship, you acknowledge fluctuating changes and respond accordingly. You are an overcomer!

You assess challenges. Rather than entertaining discouragement, you direct a path around them. Let's face it – caregiving is hard. You accept adversity acknowledging its value for personal growth. As Bernice Johnson Reagan profoundly believed, "Life's challenges are not supposed to paralyze you; they're supposed to help you discover who you are"[35]. Rather than striving against, you embrace challenges. You are an overcomer. You triumph.

The valor of caregivers is exemplified in their tenacity. With little recognition and insurmountable obstacles, caregivers remain strong as the frontline defense for their loved ones. Caregivers are a spokesperson, a friend, a comforter, an unsung hero, a difference maker. Caregivers provide hope, guidance, and encouragement. In your caregiver journey be mindful of the words penned by Leo Buscaglia. "Too often we underestimate the power of a touch, a smile, a kind word, a listening ear, an honest compliment, or the smallest act of caring, all of which have the potential to turn a life around."[36]

In a world where you are often overlooked and misunderstood, know in your soul that every day you are an extraordinary hero.

"Whenever you should doubt your self-worth, remember the lotus flower. Even though it plunges to life from beneath the mud, it does not allow the dirt that surrounds it to affect its growth or beauty."
— Suzy Kassem[37]

STEPPING STONE TEN

. . . .

Final Thoughts

THE LOTUS FLOWER, symbolic in many cultures, illustrates that even unpleasant places can produce beauty. The lotus flower is also a message for caregivers to take heart. Out of the muck and mire of caregiving, emerges a beautiful transformation of inner strength, perseverance, and resilience.

A perennial, the lotus flower flourishes in murky, nutrient-rich aquatic conditions. Rooted in mud, the stems grow up reaching the top of the water where the flower then blooms. As the lotus blooms, the petals unfold one by one. Though arising out of the muck and mire, each flower is exquisite without spot or stain. Following the rise and fall of the sun, the lotus returns to the murky water each evening and rises each morning opening their gorgeous blooms.

The lotus flower is an inspiration to caregivers. Faced with the muck and mire of confusion, anger, physical demands, emotional challenges, cognitive decline, and more, caregivers rise above, displaying exemplary endurance.

Strength. The stunning beauty of the lotus flower despite their murky, unpleasant conditions is a reminder that strength comes from enduring adversity. It is also a reminder that those things that seem unpleasant perhaps are not so since they render strength. Like the lotus flower, it behooves caregivers to know that both they and their loved one are works of art. In the swamp and out of the swamp lies opportunity to radiate beauty. Also remember that as the lotus flower retreats each night, times of rest and revitalization are imperative for strength to permeate. As Robert Schuller aptly states, "Never underestimate your problem or your ability to deal with it."[38]

Persistence. Every evening the lotus flower closes its petals and returns to the murky, swampy water. And every morning the flower emerges from the murky, swampy water with spotless, stunning beauty. And so, the cycle continues day and night. A paradigm for caregivers, the lotus flower symbolizes the persistence of caregivers. Despite constant drain and deluge, there you are persisting with exquisite tenacity. An extraordinary feat, you rise to the occasion undaunted, exhibiting stunning resolve.

Resilience. The lotus flower exemplifies resilience. Each petal of the lotus flow has a protective coating that resists dirt and water. This protective layer allows filth to easily slide off the petals leaving them to display their stunning beauty and wonder. To embrace resilience, caregivers need a protective coating. It may be grit. For some it is faith. For others it may be mindfulness or meditation. Wrap your chosen protective coating in gratitude for the honor to care for a loved one in this capacity.

Strength, courage, and resilience are not always a visible characteristic. Often, these attributes happen in the quiet unseen battles. As you go through the caregiver muck and mire, remember your shining beauty. You are strong. You are persistent. You are resilient.

ACKNOWLEDGEMENTS

Thank you to Robin Albright, Coach, Author, and Owner of Zinger Zanger, for leading me to discover my voice. You are an inspiration to me.

Thank you to James Schellenberg, The Big Picture Social Media for your valuable input, support, and nurture.

Thank you to Amber Bowcott, Walk Manager, Peoria, Decatur, and Knox-Warren, Walk to End Alzheimer's, for your review and proof drafts of the book. Your expertise and dedication are invaluable.

ABOUT THE AUTHOR

 Author, writer, and educator, Karen is passionate about helping informal caregivers navigate the mental and emotional trauma instinctive with caregiving. Arising out of her own journey of unfulfillment in the typical, well-meaning advice of adequate sleep, proper exercise, nutritious food, and social engagement, Karen's experience compelled her to search for inner peace and contentment through self-love and self-compassion. Karen is committed to helping informal caregivers to be rooted and grounded in their own self-worth as the impetus from which to live and to caregive.

After a twenty-year career in the professional business industry, Karen established Caregiver2Caregiver, a community dedicated to the inner well-being of informal caregivers. Karen is also the founder of Resonate Skincare. Formed as a means of providing tangible, healthy, wholesome facial skincare products to nourish the skin and the soul, Resonate Skincare offers a complete plant-based five-product package, in its Rejuvenate series, for an entire skincare routine

ksleeman59@gmail.com
www.Resonateskincare.com
http://www.Facebook.com/caregiver2caregiver59
Instagram@caregiver2caregiver

"Stepping Stones for Caregivers" is an incredibly uplifting and positive guide to the journey of caregiving. The book offers a refreshing and empowering perspective on the challenges caregivers face, providing practical advice and emotional support every step of the way. With its compassionate approach, it serves as a beacon of hope and encouragement for those navigating the complexities of caregiving.
BRIAN M. GORSICH, BOARD OF TRUSTEE, GREATER ILLINOIS MARKET, NATIONAL MS SOCIETY CHAIR, CENTRAL ILLINOIS COMMUNITY COUNCIL, NATIONAL MS SOCIETY

I was honored to be one of the first to read Stepping Stones for Caregivers, by Karen Leeman. I found it uplifting, encouraging and incredibly positive. The techniques Karen suggests can be utilized in many areas of our lives. Each chapter addresses positive ways to approach caregiving and self-care. I strongly encourage anyone in a caregiving position to read this book and apply these stepping stones. Whether you're caring for a young child, a person with disabilities or chronic illness and, especially, our elderly parents and grandparents. In fact, I wish I'd had this book when I was a very young woman caring for my dying mother. This book would have undoubtedly helped me handle that painful time in my life with much more love and grace. The truth is that we will all be in a caregiving situation at one or more times in our lives. Keep this book on hand and remember to care for yourself along the way.
ERIN PARKIN-WOODS, OWNER WHITE BUFFALO II

WORKS CITED

Raypole, C. (2022). Healthline. *How Many Thoughts Do You Have Each Day? And Other Things to Think About.* Retrieved from https://www.healthline.com/health/how-many-thoughts-per-day

Stringer, D. (2023). Imperfect Dust. The Story Behind "It is Well with My Soul": A History of the Beloved Hymn. Retrieved fromhttps://imperfectdust.com/blogs/news/the-story-behind-it-is-well-with-my-soul-a-history-of-the-beloved-hymn#:~:text=The%20lyrics%20of%20%22It%20is,well%2C%20with%20my%20soul.%22

The Key. *How to Use Mindfulness to Help with Caregiver Stress and Burnout.* Retrieved from https://thekey.com/learning-center/how-to-use-mindfulness-to-help-with-caregiver-stress-and-burnout#:~:text=Try%20slowing%20down%2C%20even%20when,or%20even%20your%20own%20tiredness.

Home Care. *Positive Affirmations for Caregivers.* Retrieved from https://www.homecare-aid.com/positive-affirmations-for-the-caregivers/#:~:text=Affirmations%20are%20simple%20statements%20that,you%20face%20with%20caregiving%20duties.

McGregor, K. (2023). House Beautiful. *The Real Meaning and Symbolism of the Lotus Flower.* Retrieved from https://www.housebeautiful.com/lifestyle/gardening/a45768436/lotus-flower-real-meaning/

Doman, F.(N.D.). VA Institute on Character. *No Mud, No Lotus: Boosting Resilience When Life is Tough*. Retrieved from https://www.viacharacter.org/topics/articles/no-mud-no-lotus-boosting-resilience-when-life-is-tough

ENDNOTES

1. The Carter Center(2011). Written Testimony of Former First Lady Rosalyn Carter Before the Senate Special Committee on Aging. Retrieved February 13, 2024 from https://www.cartercenter.org/news/editorials_speeches/rosalynn-carter-committee-on-aging-testimony.html

2. Burnett, F. H. (2014). The Secret Garden. Open Road Media Teen & Tween; Rei Cen edition.

3. Murphy, J (2019). *The Power of Your Subconscious Mind.* G&D Media; Original edition (January 11, 2019).

4. Frankl, V (1992). *Man's Search for Meaning.* (Young Readers Edition). Beacon Press, Boston.

5. Healthy Holistic Living. (2022, September 9). *Things that can be equally true.* [Facebook page]. Facebook. Retrieved January 16, 2024. https://www.facebook.com/search/top?q=healthy%20holistic%20living

6. Bronte, Charlotte (2018). *Jane Eyre (Unabridged).* Musaicum Books.

7. Rohr, R. (2004).Adam's Return: The Five Promises of Male Initiation. PublishDrive.

8. Pelzer, D. (2000). *Help Yourself: Celebrating the Rewards of Resilience and Gratitude.* Penguin Putnam, Inc., New York.

9. Pelzer, D. (2000). *Help Yourself: Celebrating the Rewards of Resilience and Gratitude.* Penguin Putnam, Inc., New York.

10. Retrieved December11, 2023 from https://www.goodreads.com/quotes/4142387-one-of-the-most-courageous-decisions-you-will-ever-make.

11. Coelho, Paulo (December22, 2019) Paulo Coelho Stories and Reflections *Closing cycles.* Paulo Coelho Blog. https://paulocoelhoblog.com/2019/12/22/closing-cycles1/

12   Germer, Christopher K., PhD (2009). *The Mindful Path to Self-Compassion – Freeing Yourself from Destructive Thoughts and Emotions*. The Guilford Press, New York|London

13   Spears, P. and Walker, T. (2013). *The Inspired Caregiver: Finding Joy While Caring for Those You Love*. Flowspirations LLC. Monterey, CA.

14   Fishel, R. (1987). *The Journey Within: A Spiritual Path to Recovery*. HCI.

15   Neff, K., PhD. (2015). *Self-Compassion: The Proven Power of Being Kind to Yourself*. Harper Collins.

16   Neff, K., PhD. (2015). *Self-Compassion: The Proven Power of Being Kind to Yourself*. Harper Collins.

17   Retrieved February 13, 2024 from*https://www.lyrics.com/lyric/3219436/Bob+Marley/Three+Little+Birds.*

18   Bennett, R. (2016). The Light in the Heart. Roy Bennett (November 15, 2021)

19   Retrieved February 5, 2024 from https://imperfectdust.com/blogs/news/the-story-behind-it-is-well-with-my-soul-a-history-of-the-beloved-hymn#:~:text=The%20lyrics%20of%20%22It%20is,well%2C%20with%20my%20soul.%22

20   Retrieved February 5, 2024from https://www.goodreads.com/quotes/tag/inner-peace.

21   Your Headspace Mindfulness and Meditation Experts (N.D.) *33 of the Best Meditation Quotes*. Headspace. https://www.headspace.com/meditation/quotes

22   Borysenko, J., PhD(2001). *Inner Peace for Busy People*. Hay House, Inc., California.

23   Retrieved February 13, 2024 from https://www.goodreads.com/author/quotes/14201175.Dr_Robert_Holden

24   Beattie, M. (1990) The Language of Letting Go: Short Meditations on Codependency. Hazelden Publishing

25   Karr, A. (1855). Tour Round my Garden. G. Rutledge & Co., London.

26   Pete Seeger. Turn! Turn! Turn! lyrics © Melody Trails Inc. C/o The Richmond Organizat, Melody Trails Inc.

[27] Hermann, H. (1982). *Siddhartha: A Novel translated by Hilda Rosner. Bantam, 18th Printing edition.*

[28] Dispenza, J. (2014.) *You are the Placebo: Making Your Mind Matter.* Hay House Inc., First edition.

[29] Mipham, S. (2013). *Running with the Mind of Meditation: Lessons for Training Mind and Body.* Harmony, reprint edition

[30] Your Headspace Mindfulness and Meditation Experts (N.D.) *33 of the Best Meditation Quotes.* Headspace. https://www.headspace.com/meditation/quotes

[31] Bristol, C. (1991). The Magic of Believing. Pocket Books.

[32] Speers, P. and Walker, T. (2013). *The Inspired Caregiver: Finding Joy While Caring for Those You Love.* CreateSpace Independent Publishing Platform, Kindle edition.

[33] Kuber-Ross, E. (1997). *Death: The Final Stage of Growth.* Scribner.

[34] Christopher Reeve Quotes. (n.d.). BrainyQuote.com. Retrieved January 20, 2024, from BrainyQuote.com Web site: https://www.brainyquote.com/quotes/christopher_reeve_141891

[35] Bernice Johnson Reagon Quotes. (n.d.). BrainyQuote.com. Retrieved January 20, 2024, from BrainyQuote.com Web site: https://www.brainyquote.com/quotes/bernice_johnson_reagon_127291

[36] Leo Buscaglia Quotes. (n.d.). BrainyQuote.com. Retrieved July 1, 2024, from BrainyQuote.com Web site: https://www.brainyquote.com/quotes/leo_buscaglia_106299

[37] Kassem, S. (2011). Rise Up and Salute the Sun: The Writings of Suzy Kassem. Awakened Press, First edition.

[38] Robert H. Schuller Quotes. (n.d.). BrainyQuote.com. Retrieved February 14, 2024, from BrainyQuote.com Web site: https://www.brainyquote.com/quotes/robert_h_schuller_156002